THE LIGHTHOUSES OF MAINE

Principal photography by John Penrod. Additional photography by Thomas Mitchell. Photos of Kennebec River Range, Franklin Island, Brown's Head and Whitlock's Mill Lights courtesy of the U.S. Lighthouse Society. Photos of Narraguagas, Machias Seal and Seguin Island Lights courtesy of Lighthouse Digest. Text by Wayne C. Wheeler, president, U.S. Lighthouse Society.

Edited by Tim Harrison of Lighthouse Digest Magazine, in Wells, Maine.

Cape Neddick Light Station

One of the most popular light stations in the United States, Cape Neddick is often referred to as The Nubble as it is situated on a "nubble" of an outcropping just off-shore near York. The station is rather new, by Maine lighthouse standards, having been constructed in 1875. And, it is a rather generic 1870's frame house with a generic cast iron tower nearby. Directly across from the station is a parking lot, which apparently was a good spot for young people to "park and spark" as they viewed the flashes of light. The station was automated in 1987 and transferred to the Town of York, which now maintains the area with a beautiful park, gift shop and restrooms.

Boon Island Light Station

Located six miles off York Maine, Boon Island is Maine's southern most light station and a major off-shore seacoast aid to navigation. The station, situated on a low lying wave swept rock, Boon Island, was anything but hospitable to early mariners. Several stories survive as to how the dangerous rock received the name "Boon." One tale has a ship wrecked crew building a large fire after being wrecked on the rock in 1682. The signal was seen on shore and they were rescued, a "boon" to those sailors.

It has been reported that a wooden beacon was erected on the island as early as 1799. It was washed away by a winter storm, as was a subsequent stone daymark. Finally in 1811 a 25 foot high stone tower was erected, tended by a keeper. Within the first five years three keepers resigned due to the harsh conditions and loneliness. The tower was destroyed by the sea in 1831. A 56 foot high stone tower was erected shortly after that and destroyed in 1851. The existing 137 foot granite tower was erected in 1855 and is the tallest lighthouse tower in Maine. The station was automated in 1979 and most of the buildings have been destroyed by storms.

Whaleback Light Station

In 1829 a 39 foot high stone tower was constructed on Whaleback Rock at the entrance to Portsmouth Harbor. It cost almost $20,000, which was a great deal of money in those days. The tower was poorly constructed and inspector I.W.P. Lewis stated, ". . . reflects disgrace upon the architect." The sea undermined the tower and it leaked. By 1842 the tower was in danger of collapsing. However, the new Lighthouse Board installed a new lantern on the tower in 1855. Finally, the tower was in such a deteriorated state that it was replaced by the present tower in 1872, the old tower remained alongside the new one until 1880 when it was removed.

Portland Breakwater Lighthouse

In 1855 a small octagonal wooden tower with a 5th order lens was erected at the end of the breakwater in Portland's Harbor. It cost $3,500. This first light was probably unattended. In 1875 a new metal 23 foot high tower replaced the original. It resembles an ancient Greek tower and is the only one of its kind in this country. A two room wooden keeper's house was constructed next to the tower in 1897, enlarged in 1902, and removed in 1935 when the aid was automated. The charming little tower was donated to the City of Portland in 1968.

Cape Elizabeth Light Station

This station was established in 1811 as a stone daymark. In 1828 two 56 foot high octagonal towers were constructed, 900 feet apart at a cost of $4,250. The double lights helped distinguish this station from nearby Portland Head. Cape Elizabeth was more of a coastal aid to navigation than Portland Head. In 1855 3rd order lenses were installed in the towers and these were replaced by 2nd order lenses in 1858. The stone towers remained unpainted until 1865 when the eastern tower was painted with four red horizontal bands and the west tower was painted white with a single vertical red stripe.

In 1874 the stone towers were replaced with two 67 foot high cast iron conical towers on square bases, 923 feet apart. Wooden frame houses with covered passageways were connected to each tower and a head keeper's house was constructed between the two. In 1924 the west tower was discontinued and since then both the middle keeper's house and that attached to the west tower were

razed. Today the east house is a private residence and the western tower is privately owned and associated with a modern house, at one time owned by Gary Merrill. The Coast Guard still owns the east tower and maintains a modern optic in the lantern room. An old fog signal building exists on the beach south of the east tower.

Wood Island Light Station

One of Maine's oldest light stations is on Wood Island. It was established in 1808 and rebuilt in 1839 as a white washed stone tower and again in 1858 as a 50 foot tall tower, which exists today. In 1967 the Coast Guard removed the lantern and old lens and installed a modern aero-beacon. However, after public outcry, the Coast Guard installed a new lantern room on the tower. The station was automated in 1986, one of the last to be automated in Maine. A large duplex and fog signal building remain.

Goat Island Light Station

The 28 foot high rubble stone tower was constructed on Goat Island in 1833. The present tower dates from 1859. The station was automated in 1991. The station led a rather quiet life, its claim to fame being that it often appeared on national news casts as a back drop to one of the major network's anchors reporting on President Bush when he was at his Kennebunkport home.

Portland Head

One of America's most famous lighthouses, the first built in Maine and the second authorized by the new government in 1790, Portland Head is famous among lighthouse photographers. It is certainly one of the top ten photographed in this country. The lighthouse is actually more of a harbor lighthouse, rather than a major seacoast beacon. It was completed in 1791 and was initially 58 feet high. Eventually this proved too low, so it was raised 14 feet. Then in 1864 it was raised again to 80 feet and a 2nd order Fresnel lens installed. In 1883 the tower was reduced in height and a 4th order lens installed. Then, strangely enough, in 1885 they raised the height back 20 feet to its present height of 80 feet and returned the 2nd order lens. In spite of serving faithfully, several vessels were ship wrecked in the vicinity and one, the Annie Maguire, went aground right at the foot of the tower in 1886.

Today Portland Head light station is owned by the Town of Cape Elizabeth. They have installed a gift shop in the garage and created a first class museum on the first floor of the keeper's dwelling. The lighthouse is located on the grounds of beautiful Ft. Williams State Park.

Ram Island Ledge

Another important lighthouse guiding mariners into Portland Harbor is Ram Island Ledge. Constructed between 1903 and 1905, it is one of Maine's newer lighthouses. Like Halfway Rock and a few others, it was always an unattended station, where the families lived on shore. The 98 foot high granite tower is identical to The Graves in Boston Harbor and was constructed at the same time by the same contractor, Royal Luther. The stonework alone cost 1/3 of the $83,000 appropriated for the construction. The original 3rd order lens was replaced with a modern optic in 1971 when the station was automated.

Spring Point Ledge

One of three caisson style lighthouses in Maine, Spring Point Ledge was originally constructed out in the water, marking a dangerous ledge. In 1950-51 the Army Corps of Engineers constructed a breakwater out to the lighthouse. The cast iron lighthouse was completed in 1897 and automated in 1960. Located in Fort Preble State Park, visitors can walk to the lighthouse and tour the ruins of the old fort.

Doubling Point Light

Kennebec River Stations

In 1898 the Lighthouse Service constructed several light stations along the Kennebec River to mark the way to Bath and its growing ship building industry. Although there was an unattended light at Fort Popham, the first lighthouse the mariner encounters after entering the river, and passing Pond Island, is Perkins Island, next comes Squirrel Point, the Doubling Point Range and Doubling Point Light stations. With the exception of Doubling Point Range, all the stations are of the same design; shingled, wooden, octagon towers with 5th order lenses, small frame keeper's quarters, a boat house, small barn, oil house and fog bell house. They are all located on the right (north) side of the river. The Doubling Point Range is located at an important bend in the river and shows the mariner the center of the channel as he approaches the bend. Between the Doubling Point Range and the Doubling Point Lighthouse (around the bend) is the Fiddler's Reach Fog Signal, a pyramidal wooden fog signal tended by the keeper of the range lights.

Squirrel Point Light

Perkins Island Light

Halfway Rock Lighthouse

Situated in the center of Casco Bay is the Halfway Rock Lighthouse, an important aid in directing the mariner away from a series of treacherous rocks and into Portland Harbor. The rough granite tower, about 77 feet high, was constructed in 1877 and fitted with a 3rd order lens which produced an alternating red and white flash every 90 seconds. The original fog signal was a 1,000 pound bell, followed by a reed horn in 1904 and a diaphragm horn in 1934. The station was automated in 1975 and the personnel removed. This lighthouse was an unattended station, where the families of the keepers lived ashore. The keepers took turns going ashore to visit with their families.

Doubling Point Range Lights

The Cuckolds

In 1874 a daymark was erected on this dangerous rock. But winter storms continued to destroy the aid to navigation. In 1886 a bell buoy was established off the rock to warn mariners, but it proved inadequate. Finally, in 1892 a half round brick fog signal station was constructed on the rock and furnished with a reed trumpet. A dwelling was constructed attached to the fog signal building. The lantern room and a lens was added to the fog signal building in 1907, and has produced a group flash white characteristic ever since. The station was automated in 1974. In the 1880's a winter storm washed the keeper's dwelling off the rock and into Boothbay Harbor. Today only the fog signal building, surmounted by the lantern, and a helicopter platform for servicing personnel remain.

Hendricks Head Light Station

This light station was established on a point of land at the entrance to Sheepscot Bay. It was constructed in 1829 as a tower on a stone house. The present 39 foot high brick tower and keeper's dwelling were constructed in 1875. A small bell fog signal house was also built in that year and connected to the dwelling and the tower by a covered walkway. An oil house and boat house completed the station. In 1914 the station was discontinued and sold to a private party. However, over the years the local fishermen stressed a need for a lighted aid at the location and the Coast Guard obtained permission from the private owner to place a lens in the tower, where it remains as an operational aid today. In recent years the station was purchased by new owners and completely restored.

Seguin Island

This light station, the highest above water in Maine, is also one of the most famous in Maine. The remote island is home to the only light station in Maine with a 1st order lens. Originally constructed in 1795, Seguin is the second oldest station to be established in the state. The first tower was wooden and cost $6,300, which included the keeper's dwelling. In 1819 a 30 foot high stone tower replaced the original at a cost of $2,500. The present 53 foot high granite tower was constructed in 1857 for $35,000 and it was fitted with the fixed 1st order lens presently employed. The station has had several fog signals over the years, including a bell, steam whistle, diaphone and diaphragm. Seguin was automated in 1965. In recent years a group called Friends of Seguin Island (located in Georgetown, Maine) have been caring for the property and providing tours during the summer months.

Pond Island Light Station

Pond Island Light Station was established on a small islet at the entrance to the Kennebec River in 1821, making it one of the older Maine stations. The original tower and house were constructed of slate cut from stone on the island. In 1855 a 20 foot conical brick tower with an attached wooden house replaced the original. The lighthouse was automated in 1960 and sometime after that the wooden keeper's dwelling was razed. Today only the tower with it's automated light and fog signal remain.

Pemaquid Point Light Station

One of the most beautifully situated light-houses in Maine, Pemaquid Point was established in 1827. It sits perched at the top of a series of long, almost horizontal sheets of granite. The original tower was replaced in 1835 and in the 1850's the present lantern was installed with a 4th order lens. In 1897 a small brick fog bell signal house was constructed in front of the keeper's dwelling. A tall, thin, weight tower can still be seen next to the bell house. When the weights descended they powered an automatic fog bell machine in the small house. Occasionally a cam would let loose a sledge hammer which went through a small slit in the wall and struck a fog bell hanging on the seaward side of the house.

The station was automated in 1934 and transferred to the Town of Bristol, which maintains a Fishermen's Museum in the lower portion of the dwelling. The second floor is a rental unit whose occupants act as caretakers for the property. Visitors are warned to stay clear of the long sweeps of granite as an occasional rogue wave has plucked an unwary stroller from the rocks.

Ram Island Light Station

This station is located off the entrance to East Boothbay Harbor and it is a relative new comer to the coast of Maine having been established in 1883. The tower is located just off the island and until automation and punishing storms, was connected to the island by a walkway (since fallen into the water). The station was automated in 1960 and a local Boothbay Group now maintains the old keeper's dwelling. Three goats roam the small islet and keep the grass cut.

Burnt Island Light Station

Located on a small island at the entrance to Boothbay Harbor, Burnt Island was established in 1821 when a small rubble stone conical tower attached to a dwelling was constructed. In 1858 a new lantern room and a 4th order lens were installed. In 1888 the Lighthouse Service discovered that the light was guiding vessels into the Cuckholds as they headed north into Boothbay Harbor. The beam was obscured in the direction of The Cuckholds. In 1890 the light became fixed red with white sectors showing mariners the two channels in the area. The station was automated in 1970.

Matinicus Rock Light Station

Matinicus Rock Light Station is one of Maine's most famous light stations. It is also one of the most desolate. Located some 25 miles from the nearest port, it lies midway between Monhegan Island and Mount Desert Rock and is an ideal location for a major seacoast light, although not ideal for the families who have had to reside there over the years. In 1827 the government decided to establish a light station on this barren, jagged rock, one of the most isolated on the entire Atlantic seaboard. The rock covers about thirty-nine acres at low tide and is inaccessible except during fair weather and smooth seas.

The original structure consisted of a stone dwelling with wooden towers on each end. The station displayed two fixed lights to help distinguish it from the single fixed light on Mount Desert to the north. In 1846 lighthouse inspector I.W.P. Lewis suggested that the towers be elevated (to enable a more powerful 1st order Fresnel lens to be seen at a greater distance). A new granite dwelling with granite towers was constructed. However, old style reflector systems were installed in the new towers, doing little to increase the range, which had been far less than the advertised range of 14 miles.

When the Lighthouse Board was established in 1852, Matinicus Rock was studied for improvement. Although the Board realized that improvements in the optics were needed, they had numerous stations to refit, plus they found the most pressing need to be the addition of a fog signal at this station. A study showed that Matinicus Rock experienced over 1,700 hours of fog a year. After a short period of using a fog bell, the Service installed a steam fog signal. Finally, in 1857 the two towers attached to the dwelling were reduced to the height of the roof of the house and two new granite towers were constructed separate from the keeper's house and 180 feet apart. New 3rd order Fresnel lenses, displaying a fixed white light, were installed in both towers and this double tower station remained as such well into the 20th century, the last double tower station to remain operational.

But Matinicus Rock Light Station is probably best known for Abbie Burgess. Young Abbie acted as an assistant keeper when her dad, Samuel, was ashore or off on fishing trips. She also cared for her invalid mother and three siblings. In January 1856, when Abbie was 17 years old, her father took the station boat to the mainland to obtain supplies. During his absence a raging nor'easter blew in, cutting him off from returning to the island. The storm was of such strength

Franklin Island Light Station

that the old dwelling was completely razed as the water swept over the rock. The new dwelling was flooded. For four weeks the storm raged off and on, and prevented Keeper Burgess from returning. Abbie went about caring for her family and maintaining the optics in the two towers. At one point she even rescued all but one of the hens from the chicken coop, which was destroyed shortly thereafter. During the spring of the next year, another storm lashed the station while the keeper was ashore. After a considerable amount of time the station supplies began to run low. The young son fashioned a sail to a station boat and struck out for the mainland. He wasn't seen for 21 days and the four girls and mother were reduced to hen's eggs and corn meal and were forced to seek shelter in one of the towers when the house was inundated. In later years Abbie married the son of a replacement keeper and went on to assist him tending the Whitehead Island station.

Constructed in 1804 at the entrance to Muscongus Bay, the Franklin Island station is one of the oldest in Maine. The original tower was rebuilt in 1830 as a conical stone tower and the present 41 foot tall, brick tower was constructed in 1855. In 1934 the station was automated and the personnel removed. In 1967 the keeper's house was razed. Today only the tower remains.

Rockland Breakwater Lighthouse

The first light established on the Rockland Breakwater was a small unattended minor aid to navigation. It consisted of a pair of vertical red lights which denotes an obstruction. As the Army Corp of Engineers extended the breakwater the lights were relocated to always mark the end of the breakwater. Finally, in 1901 the breakwater was completed and a keeper's dwelling with attached tower was constructed. A 4th order lens was installed along with a Reed Trumpet fog signal. In 1965 a modern optic was installed and the station was automated. In the early 1990's the Coast Guard spent a considerable sum of money to replace the slate roof with new slate, sand blast and paint the structure. The public can walk the mile long breakwater to the lighthouse, but it is not open to the public.

Indian Island Lighthouse

Located at the entrance to the Port of Rockport, Indian Island station was established in 1850 as the Beauchamp Point Light. It was discontinued in the 1860's and rebuilt in 1875 and named Indian Island Light Station after the small islet on which it is located. The station was discontinued in 1935 as an economy measure during the Great Depression and sold to a private party. Today it is a summer home and the station still contains the 36 foot square brick tower, attached to the dwelling, a barn and an oil house.

Owls Head
Light Station

Constructed in 1825 it is one of the oldest existing towers in Maine. The lantern room of the rubble stone tower may predate the formation of the Lighthouse Board, which would make it one of the few in the nation to survive the replacement of almost all the lighthouse lanterns in the 1850's, after the Board was established.

Owls Head was established to mark the south side of the entrance to Rockland's Harbor. Over the years, several types of fog signals were located at this station. The first was a bell struck by machinery powered by the tide. Then an automated weight powered bell striker was installed; this was followed by an electric siren. Today an electronic pure tone fog signal warns the mariner of Owls Head when the weather becomes "thick."

A fixed 4th order lens is still in use in the lantern room.

Over the years the keeper's dwelling was replaced and then modified. Today it is the home of a Coast Guard officer stationed in the area. There is a parking lot near the station and visitors may tour the grounds, although the tower isn't normally open to the public.

The Head got its name due to the fact that from the water the point looks like an owl's head with two caves serving as the eyes.

M A I

KENNEBEC RIVER

D'

● AMES LEDGE
● ABAGADASSET POINT
(2 LIGHTS)

GRINDEL POINT ●

● CURTIS ISLAN

● INDIAN ISLAND

DOUBLING PT.
(3 LIGHTS)

ROCKLAND
ROCKLAND BREAKWATER ●

● OWLS HEAD

HENDRICKS HEAD

SQUIRREL PT. ●

BROWNS HEAD ●

●

○ BAY

PERKINS I. ●

FRANKLIN ISLAND

● BURNT

WHITEHEAD

FORT POPHAM ●

● PEMAQUID POINT

TWO-BUSH ISLAND

AY ROCK

● RAM ISLAND

TENNANT HARBOR

● HERON

CUCKOLDS

MARSHAL POINT

POND ISLAND

SEGUIN

NO 74

● MONHEGAN ISLAND
MANANA ISLAND

◎ MATINICUS ROCK
(2 LIGHTS)

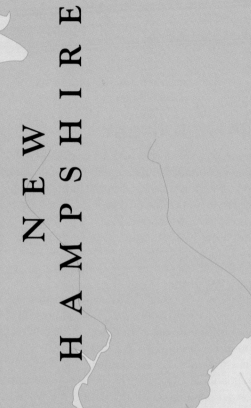

NEW HAMPSHIRE

PORTLAND

LITTLE DIAMOND

PORTLAND BREAKWATER

SPRING PT. LEDGE

CAS

RAM I. LEDGE

PORTLAND HEAD

HALF

CAPE ELIZABETH
(2 LIGHTS)

WOOD ISLAND

CAPE ELIZABETH

GOAT ISLAND

CAPE NEDDICK

PORTSMOUTH

SEAVYS I.
(2 LIGHTS)

WHALEBACK

BOON ISLAND

JAFFREY PT.

FROSTS POINT

ISLES OF SHOALS

Whitehead Light Station

Whitehead Light Station is one of the oldest stations in Maine having been established in 1802. In 1832, $6,000 was appropriated to construct the current 41 foot conical, granite tower. A new lantern was added in 1852 when a Fresnel lens was installed. Originally a bell fog signal was installed at this station. It was replaced by a steam powered whistle in 1869 and that signal was replaced by an air powered diaphragm in 1933. The station was automated in 1982 and the fog signal changed to an electronic horn. Most of the buildings of this station remain, including a schoolhouse. Maine's famous lighthouse heroine, Abbie Burgess was stationed here for many years.

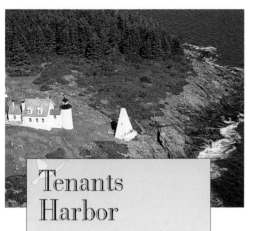

Marshall Point

Located at Port Clyde, Maine, Marshall Point was an important light station to the local fishermen and mariners engaged in the lumber trade. The station was established in 1832. The keeper's house was struck by lightning in 1894 and rebuilt around 1895 in the Colonial Revival style. The present tower, a small stone 30 foot high structure, was constructed in 1858.

After WWII the Coast Guard established a LORAN-A (electronic aid to navigation) station at Marshall Point. In the 1960's the old pyramidal fog bell house was torn down. In the 1970's the light was automated and in 1981 the LORAN station was discontinued and abandoned. Shortly thereafter the St. George Historical Society petitioned for the station and it was transferred to that Society in 1988. They spent several years restoring the old keeper's house and today the first floor is a museum dedicated to the lighthouse keepers and the local fishing industry. The second floor contains a caretaker apartment. A long gone summer kitchen was replicated next to the house. The Coast Guard still maintains a light in the tower and a small electronic fog signal.

Tenants Harbor

Established in 1857, this station served as an entrance aid to Tenants Harbor, Maine. Along with Marshall Point, Two Bush Island and Whitehead, they served as a chain of lights assisting mariners to navigate the coast into Penobscot Bay. In 1934 the Lighthouse Service closed the station and it was sold to a private party. For many years it has been owned by artist Andrew Wyeth and his wife, Betsy. Recently they gave it to their son, Jamie.

Monhegan Island Light Station

Constructed in 1824, this station is one of the important off shore light stations along the Maine coast. The gray stone conical tower originally contained a multi-lamp system backed by reflectors on a revolving frame, which produced an alternating red and white flash. This was the first use of a colored light in Maine and one of the few rotating optics in this era.

In 1850 the tower was reconstructed and in 1857 received a new lantern room and Fresnel lens.

Monhegan Island has always had a fishing village and for most of the 19th and 20th century has been a summer resort. Due to the high incidence of fog, a fog signal on Monhegan Island has been as important as the light. Because the lighthouse is on a high peak right in the middle of the island, it is not the ideal location for a signal and several locations and types of signal were used over the years.

In 1855 a 2,500 pound fog bell was established on the island and legend has it that the keeper would employ local boys to ring the bell during periods of fog or reduced visibility. In 1870 the Lighthouse Service declared the signal inadequate and established a Daboll Trumpet (steam powered) fog signal on nearby Manana Island, 1/2 mile off Monhegan Island. But this arrangement didn't prove satisfactory and a steam powered whistle signal was installed next to the Monhegan lighthouse. However, the signal was too far from the water to be effective and the Service had trouble obtaining title to suitable land near the water. So eventually the fog signal was reestablished on Manana Island. The new 8 inch steam whistle proved inadequate and the superintendent for the district reported, "The site is too low and the sound masked by neighboring hills. A better site cannot be had, on account of the difficulty of obtaining titles [to land]. It is therefore proposed to replace the whistle with a hot air trumpet raising the mouth high enough to overcome the difficulty."

Monhegan Island Light Station was one of the last to be automated in Maine and right up until automation the Coast Guard crews stationed there were also responsible for the fog signal on nearby Manana Island.

CANADA

MARKS POINT

WHITLOCKS MILL

SPRUCE POINT

ST.CROIX RIVER

PASSAMAQUODDY BAY

MIDJIC BLUFF

ST.ANDREWS
(2 LIGHTS)

PEA POINT

DREWS

BLISS ISLAND

HEAD HARBOR

CHERRY I.

WOLVES

LUBEC CHANNEL

MULLHOLLAND PT.

WEST QUODDY HEAD

AVERY ROCK

LONG EDDY

NATIONAL BOUNDARY

ABEC REACH

LITTLE RIVER

GRAND MANAN ISLAND

SWALLOW

LIBBY ISLANDS

E PEAK

SOUTHWEST HEAD

MACHIA SEAL ISLAND
(2 LIGHTS)

GANNET

TIC

AN

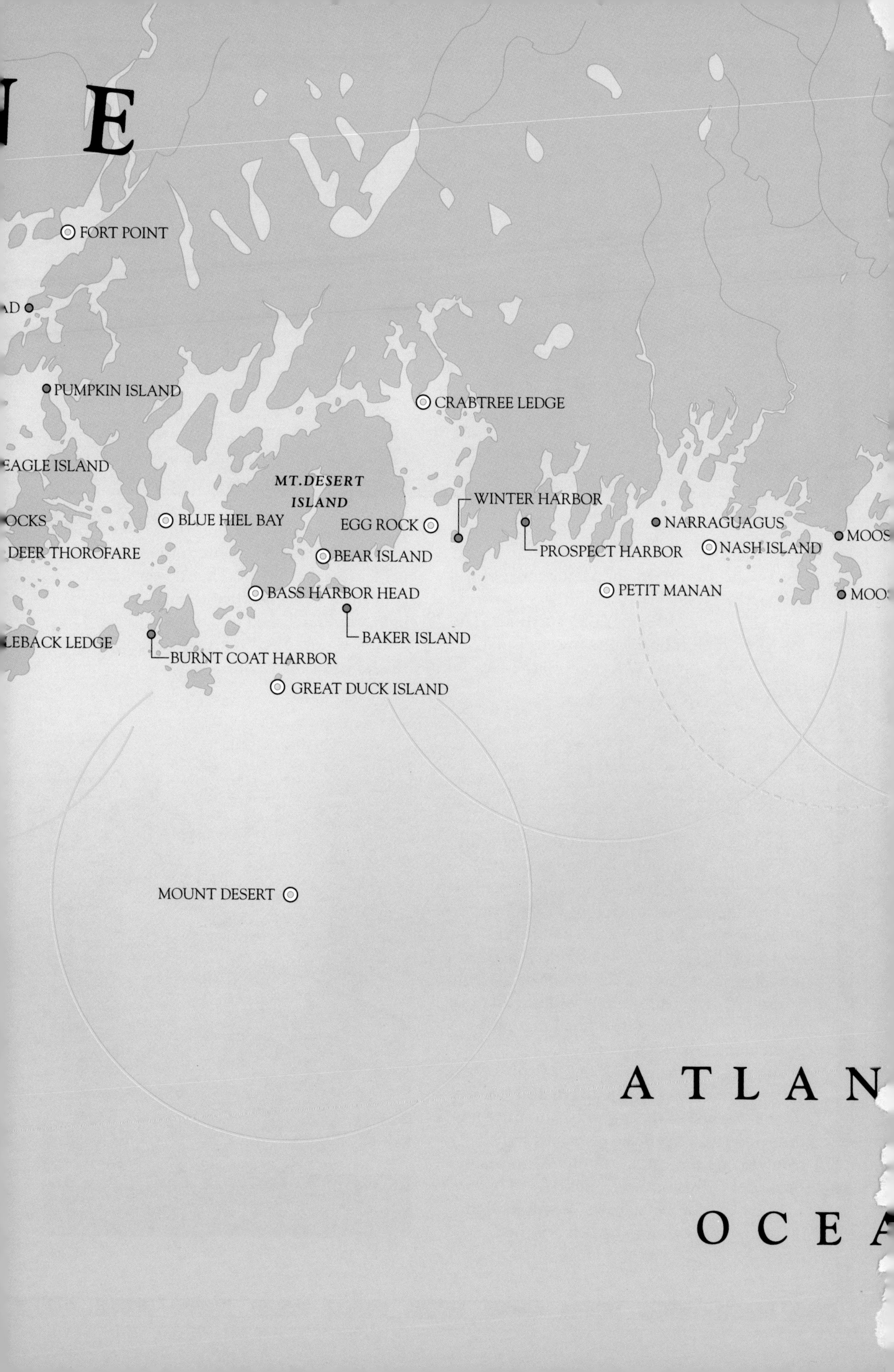

NE

FORT POINT

AD

PUMPKIN ISLAND

CRABTREE LEDGE

EAGLE ISLAND

MT. DESERT
ISLAND

WINTER HARBOR

OCKS

BLUE HIEL BAY

EGG ROCK

NARRAGUAGUS

MOOS

DEER THOROFARE

BEAR ISLAND

PROSPECT HARBOR

NASH ISLAND

BASS HARBOR HEAD

PETIT MANAN

MOOS

LEBACK LEDGE

BAKER ISLAND

BURNT COAT HARBOR

GREAT DUCK ISLAND

MOUNT DESERT

ATLAN

OCEA

Dyce's Head

Located in the quaint Maine town of Castine, the Dyce's Head station was constructed in 1829, one of Maine's older stations. The 42 foot high rubble stone tower displayed a fixed white light 130 feet above the Bay. Like all American light stations, the Dyce's Head tower received a new lantern room and Fresnel lens in the 1850's. The station was discontinued in 1937 when a small automated light was established on a nearby tower. The station is now a private residence. Castine is the home of the Maine Maritime Academy.

Fort Point Light Station

Established in 1836 near the Town of Stockton Springs, Fort Point's light guides vessels into the Penobscot River. The point is named for Fort Pownal constructed in 1758 during the French and Indian wars. The British destroyed the fort in 1779 after they defeated the colonists at Castine. Remnants of the fort can still be seen nearby along with the foundation stones of a huge resort hotel that prospered here in the 19th century.

The present square brick tower (with a circular interior) was constructed in 1857. The station was one of the last to be automated in this country. In 1988 the personnel were removed and the station transferred to Maine's Bureau of Parks and Recreation.

A rare bell fog signal tower is still located on the grounds with a fog bell attached.

Grindle Point

The Grindle Point Light Station is located at Gilkey Harbor, a port of Isleboro Township and right next to the ferry dock. The station was established in 1851 with a lantern erected on the roof of a red brick dwelling. The present 38 foot brick tower was constructed in 1874 when a 1,000 pound fog bell was installed. In 1935 the station was given to the Town of Islesboro and the light placed on a nearby tower. The town created a maritime museum in the old quarters. In 1987 the town convinced the Coast Guard to relocate their small automated light back in the tower. A small fog bell presently at the station is on loan from the Shore Village Museum in Rockland, Maine.

Curtis Island Light Station

Originally Curtis Island was called Negro Island possibly due to the first resident of the island being an African American. The station was renamed Curtis Island in the 1930's to honor Cyrus Curtis, founder of the Curtis Publishing Company of the Saturday Evening Post Fame and a noted philanthropist. The Curtis Island station, guiding vessels into quaint Camden Harbor, was established in 1839 with the erection of the present 38 foot high conical stone tower. In the 1850's the lantern room was replaced with the present lantern and a 4th order Fresnel lens was installed. The existing dwelling probably dates from the 1870's. In 1935 the light was changed from white to green, which it is today, and the station was automated. In recent years the island (and station) was licensed to the town of Camden.

Browns Head Lighthouse

Browns Head Lighthouse was established in 1832 with a short cylindrical tower attached to a crude keeper's dwelling. The station guards the eastern entrance to the Fox Island Thorofare. The Lighthouse Board rebuilt the station with a more suitable quarters and a 28 foot high brick tower in 1857. For many years a bell fog signal was sounded during periods of reduced visibility. The station was automated in 1987 and the quarters licensed to the town of Vinal Haven.

Goose Rocks

One of Maine's few caisson structures, Goose Rocks was constructed in 1890 in the channel between Vinal Haven and North Haven Islands. This is a major navigation channel between the islands and used by vessels entering Penobscot Bay from the Deer Island Thorofare and the open ocean. The channel is called Fox Islands Thorofare because North Haven & Vinal Haven used to be called North and South Fox Island.

The cast iron caisson and tower was an unaccompanied station. That is, the keeper's families lived ashore and the keepers rotated their times on and off the lighthouse. The red light has a white sector up and down channel. As the mariner approaches the lighthouse he tries to keep his vessel in the white sector, which means he is in the channel. If he sees red that means he is sailing out of the channel.

The station was automated in 1963. In recent years the Coast Guard completely refurbished the lighthouse.

Eagle Island Lighthouse

Eagle Island Lighthouse was established in 1839 when the present 35 foot high granite tower was constructed. Originally, like all American lighthouses before 1852, the optic consisted of a multi-lamp system backed by reflectors. After the Lighthouse Board was created in 1852, the reflectors were replaced with a 4th order lens (in 1858) and a new lantern was installed. A fog bell was added in the 1880's. In 1959 the light was automated, the bell discontinued and the keeper's house torn down. Today the tower supports an automated solar powered lens. The old wooden pyramidal fog bell tower can still be seen in front of the tower. Fog bell structures, such as this, are becoming a rare breed as many have been torn down over the years or are in a dilapidated condition.

Pumpkin Island

Located at the west end of Eggemoggin Reach, Pumpkin Island Light Station is situated on a small rocky islet. It was constructed in 1854 to assist mariners navigating between Penobscot Bay and various ports "Down East." The station was discontinued in 1935 and has been a private residence ever since.

Burnt Coat Harbor Light Station

The station was established on the Hockamock Head of Swans Island, off Mount Desert island, in 1872 as rear light of a range light station. However, the loss of a vessel using the range in 1885 proved the range was a hindrance to navigation. After that wreck the front light was discontinued and the front tower was later torn down. In 1977 a small automatic light was established on a steel tower on the grounds and the lighthouse discontinued. However, due to complaints of the mariners, the lighthouse was relighted in 1978 as an automated light.

The strange name apparently came about when an American chart maker took the name from a French chart which named it Brule Cote (French for Burnt Hill) mistaking the Cote for "Coat".

Saddleback Ledge

One of the wave swept coastal stations in Maine, Saddleback Ledge is a small rocky islet located between Isle Au Haut and Vinal Haven Islands. The gray granite conical tower was erected in 1839 and one of the few from that era not totally rebuilt by the Lighthouse Board. It was described by lighthouse inspector I.W. P. Lewis in his 1843 report on the state of lighthouses as, ". . . the only one ever erected in New England by an architect and engineer". The original reflector lamp system was replaced by a 5th order lens in 1856 and a 4th order lens in 1905. A lens larger than a 4th order wouldn't improve the range of the light due to the relatively short 41 foot tower.

Like many lighthouses located in major water fowl fly ways, the fixed light characteristic of Saddleback Ledge attracts birds. It is reported that in February 1927 120 birds struck the lantern on one night! Because of this, many lighthouses in fly ways have a protective screen placed around the lantern rooms. Saddleback Ledge was automated in 1954.

Isle Au Haut

Located on Robinson's Point of Isle Au Haut in the Acadia National Park, this station is one of the newer in Maine, having been constructed in 1907. In 1934 the small tower, connected to shore with a walkway, was automated and the lens downgraded to a 5th order. The Dutch Colonial keeper's house was sold to a private party. Today Jeff and Judy Burke operate the Keeper's House as a bed and breakfast inn. The house has no electricity and the meals are cooked on a wood fired stove. There are no vehicles on Isle Au Haut. Visitors reach the island and Keeper's House by mail boat.

Deer Island Thorofare

Deer Island Thorofare Lighthouse, also called Mark Island after the small islet on which it is located. The station is strategically located at the confluence of two major waterways. It was constructed in 1857 as a 4th order light, the fog signal was added in 1884. The station, which consisted of a brick tower attached to the keeper's house, caught fire in 1959. What remained of the wooden residence was removed and the tower automated. Today it displays a flashing white light and has a small electronic fog signal.

Baker Island Light Station

Baker Island Light Station was established in 1828 by order of President John Quincy Adams. It is in the Cranberry Islands and part of the Acadia National Park. The 128 acre island is heavily wooded. The present 43 foot high brick tower was constructed, along with a small keeper's house, in 1855. In 1966 the light was automated and the personnel removed.

Bear Island Light Station

This lighthouse guided mariners into Mt. Desert Island's Bar Harbor for many years. It was established in 1839 as a small house with a lantern on the roof. After the Lighthouse Board was created in 1852, they constructed a brick tower and installed a 5th order lens. The tower proved to be too small and in 1889 a new brick tower was constructed. The Coast Guard electrified and automated the light in 1961 and discontinued the station in 1981. However, the tower still displays a light which is a Private Aid to Navigation.

Bass Harbor Light Station

Right around the corner from Bear Island, on the south tip of Mt. Desert Island is Bass Harbor Lighthouse. The station was established by the Lighthouse Board in 1858 and equipped with a 5th order lens. The Lighthouse Service upgraded the lens to 4th order in 1900. Although automated in 1964, it is the residence of a Coast Guard officer who is stationed nearby and the grounds are off-limits to the public. However, there is a public parking lot and trails which enable you to take great photographs. It is a popular tourist attraction in Acadia National Park.

Blue Hill Bay Light Station

Blue Hill Bay Light Station is located on tiny Green Island and sits at the junction of several waterways. The 27 foot high tower is one of the shortest towers in New England.

The single family station was established in 1856 and automated in 1935. It is presently unlighted and a private residence.

Mount Desert Rock Light Station

Located 20 miles off the mainland and 17 miles from Mount Desert Island, is one of the most remote light stations in the country. The island is a low granite rock only 20 feet high and devoid of any vegetation. During the 19th century keepers would bring barrels of earth out to the rock from the mainland and place it in crevices. The wives would plant flowers and some vegetables in the dirt, but the first winter storm which swept over the rock would wash the dirt away. Keepers reported that seas would occasionally wash, or move, huge boulders across the rock. One was measured to be 18 feet long, 14 feet wide and 6 feet thick. On one occasion a boulder weighing about 75 tons was moved 60 feet along the rock.

The station was established in 1830 as a small wooden tower affixed to the top of the keeper's house, just 56 feet above the sea.

Eventually the service realized that a more substantial and taller, gray granite, conical tower was needed at this location. A taller tower would enable the light to be seen at a greater distance. In 1855, $10,000 was authorized for the construction of a new tower, which was completed in 1857. In 1876, a new one and a half story dwelling was constructed for additional keepers. This was required due to the establishment of the steam fog signal. In 1893 the original dwelling was replaced by a new one.

The station has been automated for several years. But members of the Fish & Wildlife Service reside on the islet, studying the numerous types of sea birds which nest there. Although automated, the Mount Desert Rock tower still flashes its warning out to sea and shows the mariner the way into Frenchman's and Blue Hill Bays.

Great Duck Island Lighthouse

One of Maine's newer light stations, Great Duck was established in 1890. Given its strategic location off Mt. Desert Island, it is amazing that this station wasn't established earlier.

The station originally consisted of a small conical brick tower, three keeper's dwellings and a fog signal building. The original 5th order lens was replaced by a larger 4th order lens in 1900. One interesting aspect of this station was the fact that the island, occupied only by the keepers and families, had its own schoolhouse. On most isolated stations either a teacher was assigned for the school year and used a room in one of the buildings for a school room, or the children boarded out ashore during the school year. But in 1902 keeper Nathan Reed arrived with 16 children. Because there were already 12 children on the island, Keeper Reed successfully petitioned for a schoolhouse, which was constructed in 1904. One of Reed's daughters, Rena, became the teacher and taught on the island. The schoolhouse was closed in 1912 when Reed departed for the Nash Island station. Today most of the buildings are gone and the small tower has an automated light. The island is now a bird sanctuary.

Egg Rock Lighthouse

In 1875 the Lighthouse Board constructed a light-house on barren Egg Rock in the center of the entrance to Frenchman Bay. The station consists of a square two story building, with a tower in the center of the roof, and a fog signal building. Egg Rock station was automated in 1976, the lantern room removed, and modern aero-beacons installed. The local mariners complained about the appearance and in 1986 the Coast Guard placed an aluminum lantern back on the tower.

Nash Island Light Station

The lighthouse is situated on a small islet located halfway between the Moose Peak and Petit Manan stations. It was established in 1838, when a 31 foot high rubble stone tower and crude keeper's dwelling were constructed. The tower was replaced by the present square 34 foot high tower in 1873 along with a new dwelling. Until 1946 the tower displayed a red light. In that year it was changed to flashing white and the 1,200 pound fog bell was discontinued. The station was discontinued in 1981, replaced by a lighted buoy off shore, and all the structures but the tower were razed.

Petit Manan Light Station

A 32 foot high rubble stone tower was constructed on Petit Manan Island in 1817. This station is one of the major seacoast stations in Maine. The technology of the Fresnel lenses, which the Lighthouse Board brought into this country in the 1850's, were superior to the reflector system they replaced. However, to enable the light to be seen further, it was necessary to construct taller towers (to reach over the curvature of the earth). Such was the case at Petit Manan. In 1855 a 119 foot tall granite tower was constructed and a 2nd order Fresnel lens installed. The characteristic was a rare FVF (Fixed white light Varied with a Flash every two minutes).

In 1869 the table holding the weights which powered the clockworks mechanism of the lens parted, causing the weights to fall and break 18 of the cast iron steps of the staircase. In 1887 the tower developed cracks due to heavy winds. Today you can see the tie rods and support cables which were installed in that year to support the thin tower. The 2nd order lens was removed when the station was automated in 1972. It is now on display in the Shore Village Museum in Rockland, Maine.

Prospect Harbor

Originally this station was established in 1848. A 35 foot high rubble stone tower displaying a fixed white light was constructed. The light was considered unnecessary for the needs of navigation and discontinued in 1865. In 1870 the Lighthouse Service changed its mind and re-established the light fitting it with a 5th order lens. The present 38 foot high wooden tower and attached keeper's house was constructed in 1891, using the old lens. The station was automated in 1934 and is presently located on Navy property.

Winter Harbor Point

Located at the entrance to Frenchman Bay, this light station was in existence from 1856 to 1934. The original conical tower attached to the keeper's house exists but it is no longer an aid to navigation. The lighthouse is now privately owned.

Narraguagus Light Station

Located on Pond Island in Narraguagus Bay this lighthouse was completed in 1856 under orders from President Franklin Pierce. When there was no longer any night travel in the area, the station was closed. It was sold in 1934 and remains privately owned.

Little River Light Station

Little River was established in 1847, when a 34-foot-tall white washed stone tower was built. In 1876 the original tower was replaced by a 41-foot-high conical iron tower painted white. In 1900 the tower was repainted brown and then in 1934 changed back to white. An automated light on a small tower replaced the light station in 1975. As the entrance to Little River is practically invisible to mariners arriving from the east, white spots were painted on rocks at the entrance in the 18th and 19th centuries. Over the years Maine had some of the most unusual aids to navigation in the nation. Fishermen and other mariners established such aids to assist them as boots hanging from a tree limb and in one case a horizontal "wheel with things hanging down." Many of these one of a kind and unusual aids to navigation became established aids and even became listed in the official Light List published by the government.

Libby Island Light Station

Libby Island Light Station, located at the entrance to Machias Bay, was constructed in 1823, but the stone tower collapsed the following year and was replaced with another rubble stone tower. In 1842 the present granite tower was constructed. A French 4th order lens was installed in 1855. The station had several different types of fog signals over the years. The first was a bell, established in 1874. In 1884 a steam powered trumpet replaced the bell and this in turn was replaced by a steam whistle in 1892. In 1923 an air-powered diaphone took over. The light and fog signal were automated in 1974.

Moose Peak Light Station

This station was constructed in 1826 when the 57 foot high brick tower was constructed. This station is considered a primary seacoast light, providing the mariner with a light with which to fix his position as he navigates along the Maine coast. A 2nd order Fresnel lens was established in the tower in 1856. This is one of the larger Fresnel lenses in Maine, only the 1st order lens on Seguin Island is larger. The crude original keeper's dwelling was replaced by a Dutch Colonial duplex in the 1870's. The station was automated in 1972.

Lubec Channel Lighthouse

Constructed in 1890, this cast iron tower on a steel caisson was one of 47 of this type constructed in America the latter years of the 19th century and early years of this century. This style light station is often referred to as a "sparkplug." It was an unaccompanied station where the keeper's family lived ashore. Usually there were three keepers assigned to this type of station, with one spending every third day on shore. The station was automated in 1939 and the personnel removed after a fire severely damaged the station. In 1989 the Coast Guard announced they were going to raze the structure due to the cost of restoring it. When the local citizens objected, the service stated they would move the tower portion to shore. The Maine Historic Preservation Commission enabled the Coast Guard to leave the structure in place and restore it for $700,000.

Whitlocks Mill Light

Whitlocks Mill Light is a Johnny-Come-Lately station, constructed in 1910 and located along the St. Croix which divides America from Canada. Originally the aid was a small unmanned lantern hung from a post in 1892. The present brick tower was constructed in 1910 along with the keeper's house, now a private residence. The station was automated in 1969.

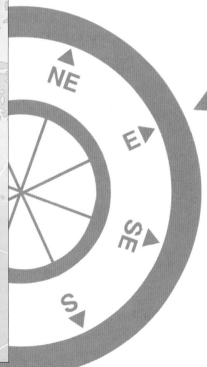

West Quoddy Head

West Quoddy Head is one of the more famous light stations in Maine, probably because of the red and white candy stripes. The station is also the easternmost lighthouse on the mainland of the United States. The first tower of the West Quoddy Head Light was a 59-foot-tall wooden white washed structure constructed in 1808. The present tower was constructed in 1858, and its 15 red and white stripes are unique in America. America's first fog signal, a bell, was established at this station in 1820. West Quoddy Head Light Station, still displaying a Coast Guard light, is presently managed by Maine State Parks Department. It was automated in 1988.

East Quoddy Head Light Station

This Canadian station, also known as Head Harbour Light, is located on the east end of Campobello Island, in New Brunswick, right across from the American West Quoddy Head Station. Like most Canadian stations it is painted red and white, but it does sport a distinctive red cross on the tower. The original 1829 tower was replaced with the present structure in 1885.

Mulholland Lighthouse

Located on the east side of the Lubec Channel, this typical Candian station can be easily viewed from Maine. The tower was erected in 1885 and donated to the Roosevelt Campobello International Park in 1985. Long automated, only the tower of the station remains and is no longer a functioning aid to navigation.

Machias Seal Island

This two island group is the subject of a long running dispute between Canada and the U.S., both countries claim the islands. To prove their right to the islands the Canadian Coast Guard mans the light station on one of the islands. The station was first established in 1832. The present tower was constructed in 1878 and is typical of the Candian towers, white with a red lantern room. The island is home to a large colony of puffins and other sea birds.